THE VALUE OF SHARING

The Story of the Mayo Brothers

VALUE COMMUNICATIONS, INC.
PUBLISHERS
LA JOLLA, CALIFORNIA

THE VALUE OF SHARING

The Story of the
Mayo Brothers

BY SPENCER JOHNSON, M.D.

First Edition
Manufactured in the United States of America
For information write to: ValueTales, P.O. Box 1012,
La Jolla, CA 92038

Library of Congress Cataloging in Publication Data

Johnson, Spencer.
    The value of sharing.

    (ValueTales series)
    SUMMARY: The Mayo brothers, knowing the importance of sharing, enter a career in which they can share their knowledge, skills, and money with sick people and other doctors.
    1. Mayo, Charles Horace, 1865-1939—Juvenile litera-ture. 2. Mayo, William James, 1861-1939—Juvenile literature. 3. Surgeons—Minnesota—Rochester—Biogra-phy—Juvenile literature. [1. Mayo, Charles Horace, 1865-1939. 2. Mayo, William James, 1861-1939.
3. Physicians. 4. Sharing] I. Title.
RD27.35.M38J63   610'.92'2[920] [B]   78-10578

ISBN 0-916392-28-7

This tale is about two brothers who shared many things together. The story that follows is based on events in their lives. More historical facts about the Mayo Brothers can be found on page 63.

Once upon a time...

not so very long ago, there were two young brothers named Will and Charlie Mayo.

Will and Charlie lived in a little town in Minnesota, where their father was a country doctor. They loved to ride out across the prairies with him when he made his calls. They were proud and happy whenever the busy doctor helped a sick person feel well again.

But Dr. Mayo couldn't always help. Once when the boys came home after they had been out with their father, they felt very sad.

"What's the matter?" their mother asked.

"Last week Dad operated on a boy to try to save his life," said Charlie. "Well, Dad couldn't save him."

"He got an infection," Will added, "and Dad couldn't stop the infection."

8

The doctor came in then, and he sat down. He looked very tired. "It's so hard to stop infections," he sighed. "If only I knew how to keep them from starting."

"Just a minute," said Mrs. Mayo. "I have to get something. I'll be right back." And she went out smiling.

Why do you suppose she was smiling at a time like this?

Why, she was smiling because she had just thought of a way to help her husband.

Dr. Mayo had asked his wife to read all the medical journals he received and to let him know about new things that might be important to him. Now she remembered something she had read. She came back in a few minutes with a journal. "Look at this!" she said to her husband.

The doctor began to read. "Wonderful!" he exclaimed. "A man named Louis Pasteur has proved that germs cause infections."

He put down the journal. "Oh, if only I could go to New York!" he cried. "I could study Pasteur's methods there! But we don't have enough money for that."

"We do have the money!" insisted his wife. "We have our savings. If it's important for you to learn about Pasteur's work, we'll go to New York!"

And so the Mayo family set out on a journey of more than a thousand miles.

In New York, Dr. Mayo joined other doctors who were working at Bellevue Hospital. He used a microscope to study the germs that cause infections. He learned that germs can't live in very clean places, and that boiling things in hot water can kill the germs that are on them. Most important, he learned what to do to stop germs from causing infections during an operation.

Dr. Mayo shared what he learned with his wife and the boys. "We're making wonderful progress!" he said. "But I should have new medical equipment. Especially a microscope. If only microscopes didn't cost so much money!"

"If you should have it, you'll have it," decided Mrs. Mayo. "We can borrow money on our house, and you can buy whatever you need to help the people you see in Minnesota."

That is exactly what Dr. Mayo did. And before long, the Mayo family returned to their home in Minnesota.

Will and Charlie danced with excitement when their father carried the microscope into the house. They could hardly wait for him to put it down.

"Why does it have such a funny name?" asked Charlie.

"Because 'micro' means 'very small,'" said their father. "'Scope' means 'to look at.'"

"I see," said Will. "So we can use it to look at very small things like germs, right?"

"Exactly," said Dr. Mayo. "But look carefully. That's a very expensive piece of equipment."

The boys were careful, and they learned to use a microscope before most other children learn the multiplication tables.

There was another thing they did while they were still very young—a thing that surprised many people. What do you think it was?

They often watched their father operate, and they helped him when they could.

There was no hospital in southern Minnesota at that time, so Dr. Mayo often performed operations on kitchen tables. The boys were so small that they had to stand on wooden boxes to see what their father was doing. And even though they were young, their dad talked to them as if they were grown. He shared his knowledge with them and explained exactly what was going on.

Most of the time the boys were proud to be helping their father, but sometimes they didn't pay strict attention. They were like most children, after all, and at times they daydreamed a bit.

It was during one of those daydreaming times—when their father was operating and talking to them, and they weren't paying much attention—that something very odd happened. A pair of ordinary surgical scissors suddenly seemed to have two twinkling eyes, which were staring straight at the boys.

"I must be seeing things!" thought Will.

"That pair of scissors is looking at me," Charlie said
to himself.

And then something even stranger happened!

The scissors began to talk!

"Hi, boys!" it seemed to say. "My name is Tu Sides and I'd like to be your friend."

"Wow!" thought the boys, "that would really be neat."

Then they seemed more than a little puzzled. "How come you're called Tu Sides?" they asked. "That's a funny name."

"Not for me," said the scissors. "Have you ever seen scissors that could cut with only one blade? Of course not. Each side has to help the other. That's called sharing. It's also called cooperation and working together, but I like to think of it as sharing.

"Your dad is sharing right now," Tu Sides went on. "He's explaining this operation to you. So he's doing his part, isn't he? What about you? Are you doing your part? Are you paying attention?"

The boys were silent for a moment. They knew they hadn't been listening to their father. "I see," said Will at last. "There are two sides to sharing. One is giving and the other is receiving."

"It's like talking and listening," said Charlie.

But before Tu Sides could say anything, Will and Charlie heard a very real voice. "Boys!" their father shouted. "Please! Pay attention!"

Will and Charlie jumped. They saw that their father had been waiting for Will to hand him an instrument. Charlie hurried to take the instruments out of boiling water and put them on the table near Will.

"Sorry, Dad," said Will. "I'm afraid we were daydreaming." And he handed Dr. Mayo the instrument he wanted.

After that, the boys remembered what Tu Sides had said.
They listened very carefully while their father explained the
rest of the operation to them.

But when they weren't watching their father, Will and
Charlie weren't always so attentive. Sometimes they didn't
listen well at school. In fact, they were only average
students. Their teachers probably never imagined that they
would grow up to become two of the most famous doctors in
the world.

23

Will and Charlie soon became close friends with Tu Sides, and they took him everywhere with them.

"We think you're nice," said Charlie. "And we like the things you say about sharing. How would you like to go to the circus with us?"

"Great!" cried Tu Sides. "I can't think of anything I'd like to share more than a circus." And so the three went off to look at the elephants and tigers and all the other circus animals.

When Will and Charlie and Tu Sides reached the big circus tent, little Charlie saw something that puzzled him.

Can you guess what it was?

Clown after clown was scrambling to get out of a tiny house.

"I don't understand," said Charlie. "Where are they all coming from?"

Before Will or Tu Sides could answer, the boys heard their mother calling to them from outside the circus tent. "Will!" cried Mrs. Mayo. "Charlie! Come quickly! Your father wants you!"

The boys forgot about the circus as they raced off to meet their father at the home of the town blacksmith.

26

"Can you help my wife, Doctor?" the man was saying as the boys came in. "Her stomach is very big and she's in a lot of pain. I'm afraid she's going to die!"

Dr. Mayo put his arm around the man. "There now," he said kindly. "You and I can work together to help save her."

"Me?" said the blacksmith. "Work with you? But I'm not a doctor. What can I do?"

"You're a blacksmith," said the doctor. "You can take a piece of metal and heat it in the fire. Then you can pound it into any shape you like.

"I'm going to need special instruments for your wife's operation. She has a tumor growing deep inside her, and the instruments I have aren't long enough. You can make the instruments I need to reach the tumor."

28

Of course the blacksmith set to work right away, with the boys and Tu Sides watching.

While the blacksmith hammered at the metal, Dr. Mayo talked with the sick woman. "We're going to help you," he promised. "My boys are here now, and my wife will come with other doctors who will assist with the operation. You'll be all right. You'll see."

When Mrs. Mayo and the doctors arrived, the room was ready. Everything was as clean as it could be before Dr. Mayo began the operation.

"You see," said Tu Sides, "your father remembers what he's learned. He's doing everything he can to keep an infection from starting."

"Wouldn't it be terrible if his teachers hadn't shared with him," said Will. "What would happen if people didn't share what they know with one another?"

"We'd have to learn everything from scratch," said Charlie.

When the operation was over, Dr. Mayo talked to the blacksmith. "Your wife is going to be just fine," he said.

When the boys saw the blacksmith's happy smile, they knew that they, too, wanted to be doctors to help people like their father did.

"Of course you can be doctors," Mrs. Mayo said when they told her. "You can be good doctors—and the more you know about people and their feelings, the better you'll be."

"I'm glad you're reading Charles Dickens' stories," said Dr. Mayo to Will. "Dickens knows a lot about people and how they feel."

31

As he grew up, Will learned that it took more than reading to become a doctor. He had to work and make money so that he could go to medical school.

Will got a job working in a drug store after school. He swept and dusted. He also learned how to make all kinds of medicine. And he saved his money.

One evening, when he was almost ready to leave for medical school, he didn't go straight home after work. He headed for the general store. And there he met his mother and father and Charlie.

"Now what?" said Tu Sides.

"Now I'm going to buy Charlie a new suit," said Will. And he did!

"I can't believe it!" Charlie said as he stared at himself in the mirror. "A new suit! Brand new! I've never had a new suit!" He gave his brother a big hug.

"I figured you must be pretty tired of always wearing my old clothes," said Will. He was smiling proudly.

"It feels good, doesn't it, when you share with someone," whispered Tu Sides.

33

Will took Tu Sides with him to medical school. He followed Tu Sides' advice, too. When his teachers were talking, he listened and learned. And of course he always shared what he learned with his brother Charlie when he went home.

After many years of hard work, Will graduated from medical school. He was happy to be able to help his father care for sick people all over the county. Everyone in town began to call him Dr. Will.

"Gee, Will," said Charlie, "now I can drive around with you, just the way we used to go around with Dad."

Charlie was very proud of his brother Dr. Will.

One hot summer day, Charlie and Dr. Will had been out seeing patients in the country. They stopped the carriage when they noticed that the sky was growing dark. The wind had stopped, and everything was strangely quiet.

"What is it?" whispered Charlie. He sounded scared.

"Look!" Will pointed. "A tornado!"

Charlie saw a funnel-shaped cloud off in the distance.

"Hee-up!" cried Will, and he whipped the horse into action. "We'll be safer in town!" he cried.

But Will was wrong. As they raced over a wooden bridge
and onto the main street of town, the tornado roared down
after them.

Charlie and Will reached the far side of the bridge just an
instant before the vicious wind hurled the bridge up into the
air. Timbers shattered into chips and pieces as they smashed
to the ground near the two brothers.

The brothers were blown out of their carriage when the wind
screamed past them. They were swept down the main street
of Rochester like two leaves blown from a tree.

The tornado raced through the town. It smashed buildings
and tossed the wreckage into the air. Then, as suddenly as it
had come, the storm sped away across the countryside.

Charlie and Will had been blown up against a building. They
looked around, amazed. Somehow they had not been hurt.
But there were lots of injured people all around them.

Dr. Will and Charlie set to work helping the people who were hurt. Dr. Mayo came running. The town hall was turned into an emergency hospital. Temporary beds were set up. A group of nuns acted as nurses, and everyone else in the town pitched in and helped.

But the town hall wasn't very clean. Some of the wounded people got infections. Some died.

"We need a hospital," said one of the sisters after the tragedy was all over. "We need a place where we can take care of people who are sick or hurt."

"Indeed we do," agreed Dr. Mayo.

"We'll raise the money and build the hospital," said the sisters, "if you and your sons will be the doctors."

"What a great idea!" cried Dr. Will. "Charlie is going to medical school soon. When he finishes, there'll be three Mayo doctors to share the work that has to be done."

Tu Sides grinned. "That's another good thing about sharing," he said. "It makes the work easier."

It took a long time to build the hospital. But, then, it took a long time for Charlie to become a doctor. While he studied, Dr. Will and Dr. Mayo took care of people. Sometimes their patients paid them with a chicken from the hen house. Sometimes they paid with a basket of apples from the orchard. Sometimes they couldn't pay at all.

"Don't worry," Dr. Will always said. "We only want to help you get better."

42

When Charlie came home from medical school, he found that many patients were coming to his father and his brother for help. And he laughed the first time one of the patients called him "Dr. Charlie."

"That sounds pretty good," he said to Tu Sides.

After the hospital was opened, the three Mayo doctors were able to help even more people. Dr. Will and Dr. Charlie had learned the newest and best methods of scientifically treating patients. Their father, however, knew also how important it was for a good doctor to be aware of patients' feelings, too.

"Never forget that we're taking care of people," he would say, "and there's more to pay attention to than just their sickness."

Soon people were coming to the Mayos from all over Minnesota. "The Mayo doctors are good at their work," said these patients. "Their surgical rooms are clean. They use carbolic acid to kill the germs. Almost no one ever dies because of infection at the hospital in Rochester."

Before long, patients weren't the only people who came to see the Mayos. Can you guess who else came?

Doctors and nurses from nearby towns came. They wanted to see just how the Mayos were able to help so many people.

"That's very funny!" said Tu Sides. "You used to stand on boxes to watch your dad operate. Now other doctors are standing on boxes to watch *you*!"

"If they can learn from us, we're glad," said Dr. Will.

"We're always happy to share what we know with others," declared Dr. Charlie.

But the Mayo brothers realized that there were things they
didn't know—things they had to find out. "Why don't you
and I take turns traveling?" said Will to Charlie one day.
"One of us can stay at home and look after our patients
while the other visits the best hospitals and the best doctors
in the world. Then the one who's been traveling can come
home and share what he's learned. That way we can keep
learning and be better doctors."

Dr. Charlie thought that was a great idea, and from that time
on the Mayos traveled all over the world learning more and
more about medicine.

You could see one of the Mayo brothers at almost any big meeting of doctors. And they were easy to recognize. Will and Charlie didn't try to impress the other doctors by wearing fancy clothes or growing important-looking beards. But in spite of their simple, easy ways, the Mayos *did* impress the other doctors.

Everyone listened carefully whenever Charlie or Will spoke at a meeting. Why? Because the two young men from Minnesota had proved that they could prevent infections, and that they could do many types of operations very well. More people got better in the little town of Rochester, Minnesota, than in just about any other place in the world.

"My brother and I would be glad if you'd come to our clinic whenever you want," Dr. Charlie always told the other doctors. "Perhaps if we all share what we know, we can all learn something that will help our patients."

Charlie always talked in a slow, friendly way. He sounded a lot like his famous friend Will Rogers. And also like Will Rogers, Charlie Mayo had a good sense of humor. "One nice thing about sharing knowledge," he said to Tu Sides' delight, "is that after you give it to someone else, you still have it!"

Doctors from all over the world accepted Charlie's invitation. They came to Rochester to see how he and Will worked. There were no wooden boxes in the operating rooms now. Instead there were mirrors over the operating tables, and there were seats so that the visiting doctors could be comfortable as they looked up into the mirrors to see exactly what was going on. The seats could slide from one side to another, so that the visitors could move when Will and Charlie moved during an operation.

The fame of the Mayo brothers spread. Surgeons were coming from Europe and South America to spend weeks watching Will and Charlie, learning what they knew.

After their father, Dr. Mayo, was seventy, he left most of the
work at the hospital to Dr. Will and Dr. Charlie. At last his
patients were well looked after, and he had time to do
something else that he had always enjoyed doing. What do
you suppose that was?

Dr. Mayo liked to travel. In fact, he liked to travel so much that he and his wife went twice around the world the year he was eighty-seven!

Most of the time Dr. and Mrs. Mayo traveled just for fun. But when he was in far-off lands, the old doctor sometimes visited other doctors and saw their hospitals. And whenever he saw something new that might help people, he told Will and Charlie about it as soon as he got home.

Back in Rochester, things were getting pretty crowded at the little building the Mayos used for a clinic.

"Look at all those people," Dr. Will said one day when the waiting rooms were especially full. "There seem to be more people every day."

"We really need a bigger clinic," said Dr. Charlie.

"I want to talk to you about that," said Dr. Will. "Come on into my office. You can come too, Tu Sides."

"We have a lot of money these days," said Dr. Will when they were in his office. "We've never turned anyone away because he had no money. None of our patients has ever had to borrow money to pay our bills. And still we have all this money."

"It's more than we need to live on," said Dr. Charlie.

"It surely is," agreed Dr. Will. "And it doesn't seem to me that the purpose of our clinic is to make money. It's to take care of people. So why don't we find a way to share the money with people who are sick?"

"We can build a new building," said Dr. Charlie.

"Of course!" said Will. "And then we can help support young doctors who want to study with us."

"Great!" cried Tu Sides. "You've grown into men who really know the value of sharing!"

The Mayo brothers did build a larger clinic. Then, for twenty more years they kept saving. One dollar out of every two they made was saved and invested to share later with people that were ill. When they felt they had enough, the brothers went to see the head of the University of Minnesota.

"My brother and I now have two million dollars," Dr. Will told the university president. "We'd like to give it to the university to help students and young doctors who want to study medicine at our clinic."

"What a wonderful gift," said the surprised man. "But why are you doing this?"

"Sometimes people don't understand," said Dr. Charlie. "But it is really very simple. It makes us feel good when we share what we have with others."

Can you imagine how proud Tu Sides felt?

He was prouder still when young doctors came from all over the world to study at the Mayo Clinic. Most of them stayed for three years and then went back to their own hometowns. Others stayed on to help out at the clinic.

"It's great!" said Dr. Charlie. "More and more doctors are helping more and more people."

All through this busy, happy time, there was one person who was prouder of the Mayo brothers than anyone else. She had watched the two little Mayo boys grow up into two fine men. Can you guess who she was?

It was their mother!

Mrs. Mayo was over eighty, and she still read the medical journals, just as she had read them for her husband. But now she looked for articles by Dr. Will Mayo or Dr. Charles Mayo. And often she found such articles, for her sons shared their knowledge by writing more than a thousand papers for the medical magazines.

They had never been interested in fame, but the Mayo brothers had become famous. They were honored everywhere. Even the President of the United States was proud to talk with the Mayos.

But Dr. Will and Dr. Charlie were quiet, humble men. "I feel uncomfortable when people treat me as if I were special," Dr. Will always said. And Dr. Charlie declared that the biggest reason they succeeded was that they picked the right parents.

But the boys remembered what Tu Sides always said. Sharing is more than giving; sharing is receiving, too. So the Mayo brothers accepted the praise and the honors, and they were grateful.

No matter how many honors they warmly received, the Mayo brothers' greatest joy came from something else. It came from seeing some of the very best doctors in the world come to the little town of Rochester. Some of them stayed on in order to be a part of the Mayo Clinic. Today, people still come from all over the world to be helped by the doctors at the clinic.

The Mayos shared their knowledge, their experience, and their money. They always felt happy when they saw the good that came from their sharing.

Of course not everyone has the same things to share. You may not have much money and you probably don't have a microscope. You may not even want to share what you have with anyone. That is for you to decide. But if you do choose to give something to someone else, or to accept what others are giving to you, you may just discover something very important about yourself.

61

You may discover that sharing makes you feel happy, just as it did our good friends the Mayo brothers.

The End

The Mayo Brothers were able to share a great many things with each other during their lifetimes. They were the only two boys of five children born to Louise Abigail Wright and William Worrall Mayo. While the boys enjoyed their sisters, Gertrude, Phoebe, and Sarah, the brothers were drawn to each other in a very special way.

The boys' father was born in England and came to America in 1845 at the age of 26. After graduating from the University of Missouri Medical School in 1854, marrying, and having three daughters, he settled in the pioneer village of Le Sueur, Minnesota. There he became of the proud father of his first son, Will. As a doctor for the Army, near the end of the Civil War, Dr. Mayo, Sr. moved his family in 1863 to the site of the district recruiting station in Rochester, Minnesota, where his second son, Charlie, was born. It was here that he was to share his medical knowledge with his sons, and they with the world.

Will and Charlie grew up at the same time that surgery itself was growing up. Charlie Mayo was born in 1865, the same year that Sir Joseph Lister first announced the success of his "carbolic spray" method for controlling surgical infections. Louis Pasteur was still trying to convince most of the medical world that germs were actually the cause of infection.

A year after Charlie's birth, the clinical thermometer first came into use and three years later the first (wooden) stethoscope was introduced.

Dr. Mayo Sr., then nearly 52 years old, was determined that he and his boys would grow with the medical times. In 1871 he left his remote Minnesota village to update his knowledge and skills at New York's Bellevue Hospital. He became one of the first doctors in the country to use a microscope in his practice.

It seemed natural that both boys would become doctors. Will graduated from the University of Michigan Medical School in 1883 and Charlie from Chicago Medical School in 1888. One year later, St. Mary's Hospital opened with forty beds and three Mayo physicians—a 70-year-old father and his two sons. And, as we know, their nearby medical offices became the beginning of a cornerstone in medicine—The Mayo Clinic.

WILLIAM JAMES MAYO   1861–1939
CHARLES HORACE MAYO   1865–1939

The Mayo brothers were scientists and humanitarians. They published over 1,000 scientific papers about their work in the medical journals. What they didn't tell many people, however, was what they did behind the scenes for the less fortunate people they cared for. As many as 30 percent of their patients were surprised and relieved to find the handwritten words PAID IN FULL on the Mayos' bills—bills which they could not otherwise afford. And regardless of how much money the patients had, no one was ever charged more than 10 percent of his or her annual income, no matter how expensive the treatment. And every dollar they collected on bills over $1,000.00 went to help other sick people.

They were very close during their more than seventy years of life. And they were almost inseparable in death. When Dr. Charlie unexpectedly died of pneumonia on May 26, 1939, Dr. Will who was already ill, became lonely and lost. Without his brother and teammate, life didn't seem as important to him. Dr. Will died quietly on July 28, 1939—only two months after Dr. Charlie.

As successful as they had been as surgeons, it has been said that their real success was probably as brothers. Whenever one of them was singled out for an honor by a medical society, a university, or a government, they would each begin to accept any honor with the same four words, "My brother and I . . . ."

The ValueTale Series